TOTALLY WEIRD

Insects

Contents

Tricky words are explained on page 32.

TWO CAN ™

LONDON ■ PRINCETON

www.two-canpublishing.com

D1335702

Insects rule!

Insects live everywhere! From jungles and deserts to mountains and streams, there's no getting away from them. Scientists believe that there are up to ten million different types of insects, and every year thousands more are discovered.

Buggy bodies

Insects come in many shapes and sizes, but they have several things in common — a tough shell, six legs, and a body that's split into three parts. These parts are the head, the middle section called the thorax, and the abdomen where food is digested. Most insects also have wings and a pair of feelers, called antennae.

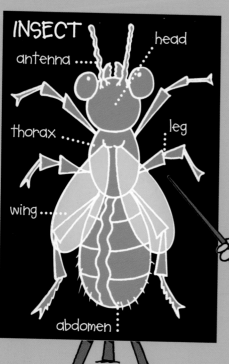

INSECT
antenna
head
thorax
leg
wing
abdomen

2

Success story

Insects have been on Earth for more than 400 million years — even longer than dinosaurs. The first creatures to grow wings and fly were insects. They took to the air to search for food and to escape from enemies on the ground.

I'm out of here.

Sorry guys. It's a private party.

INSECTS ONLY

Not in the club

What do centipedes, mites, snails, spiders, ticks and woodlice all have in common? For a start, NONE of them is an insect! The clue is that insects always have six legs.

Believe it or not

Some katydids ooze poison from the joints in their legs and aim it at enemies. Yuck!

▲ This amazing-looking alien is a type of large bush cricket, called a katydid. Its strange name comes from the chirping song that some katydids make — "katy-did, katy-didn't!"

Making sense

Insects are supersensitive creatures. Many have fine hairs that can sense tiny movements in the air, and some have huge eyes that can see in lots of directions. An insect's long antennae are excellent smelling and feeling tools.

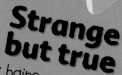

Strange but true
Tiny hairs on a fly's body act as an alarm. When danger approaches, the hairs twitch, warning the fly to zoom off.

Tuning in
The male emperor moth uses its giant antennae to pick up smells, just as a TV antenna tunes into stations. The moth's antennae are so sensitive that they can smell another moth up to 13 kilometres away.

Keeping in touch
A cave cricket doesn't need a torch to see in its dark home. It has two extremely long antennae that help it to feel its way around the cave. The cricket sweeps its antennae across the floor and along the walls to check for uninvited guests.

Uh-oh! That wasn't here yesterday.

Sounds weird

Don't look for an insect's ears on its head! Some fluttery lacewings have ears on their wings, while a cricket's ears are near its knees.

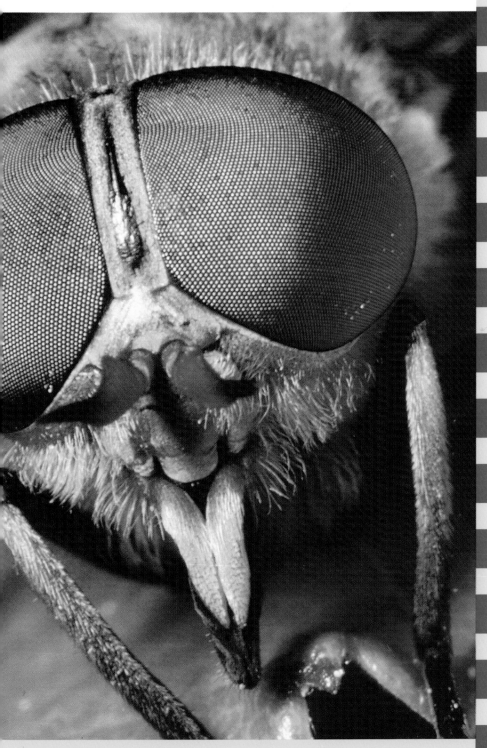

▲ A horsefly's giant eyes are made up of thousands of smaller eyes that point in many directions. The fly can even see behind itself!

Oh, it's you Fred. Hello.

Many ants have poor eyesight so they rely on smells to recognize other ants from the same nest. They sniff each other with their antennae. Ants also let off an odour to warn nest-mates of danger.

scent

Some cunning crickets cover themselves in ant scent and then sneak into ants' nests. The smelly disguise fools the unlucky ants — and they end up as the crickets' dinner!

Beetle-mania

ARMOUR PLATED

There are thousands of weird and wonderful beetles scattered all over the world, from steamy rainforests to sweltering deserts. All members of this vast insect group have extra-tough shells.

▲ This glittering golden beetle lives deep in the rainforests of Costa Rica. Many beetles come in shimmering reds and greens, but golden beetles, such as this one, are less common.

Nifty noses

This beetle has a sensational snout! The nosy fellow from Madagascar belongs to a group of big-nosed beetles, called weevils. Its supersnout is tailor-made for drilling into the weevil's favourite snacks of tasty fruits, nuts, wood and scrumptious leaves.

That's weird

A darkling beetle gets a head start to the day in the hot, dry desert. It waits for the morning dew to form on its body, then does a headstand. The droplets roll down the grooves on the beetle's back and into its open mouth.

Heavy stuff

A male African Goliath beetle is the heaviest insect — weighing in at over 80 grams — and it really likes to throw its weight around! This bruiser wrestles with other male beetles to compete for a female.

HEE HEE!

How do bees get to school? They take a buzz.

HA HA!

Up, up, and away!

▲ Like all beetles, this long-horned beetle has a pair of hard wing cases. They help the beetle to balance in the air and protect its delicate wings underneath.

Fasten your seatbelts...
We have liftoff

Most insects have wings and are expert flyers. Thes insects take off without a runway, zoom around at great speed and perform all kinds of stunts in the air. A few insects are also fancy on their feet.

Topsy turvy

A fly can turn its world around by walking up walls and hanging upside down from ceilings. Sticky pads on the fly's feet act like suction cups so the fly doesn't fall off.

Fair-weather flyers

Due to cold weather, most insect flights will be delayed until further notice! Insects, such as butterflies, hate the cold because it means they're temporarily grounded. Before they can take off, they have to sit in the sun or beat their wings to warm up.

Believe it or not

Every winter, Canadian monarch butterflies flee the cold by flying all the way from Canada to Mexico.

Under the microscope

A butterfly's beautiful wings are made up of hundreds of tiny scales that overlap in the same way as scales on a fish.

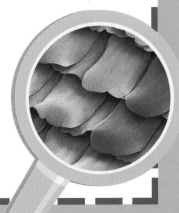

Dodge or drown

When it starts to rain, a few insects move like bumper cars, weaving in and out of the falling raindrops to avoid a soaking. Wet weather is a serious problem for small insects who can drown in just one or two raindrops.

An ideal home

Insects are ingenious at finding places to live. Their homes include leaves, paper nests and animal fur. Some insects, such as termites, build gigantic homes where millions of them live together.

Paper palaces

Wasps make paper walls for their nests. The clever workers chew wood until it turns into soggy balls of paper. Then the wasps spit out these mushy balls and use them to build their homes.

Keep on chewing, kid.

Sleepyheads

Many insects hunt for a cosy, quiet place to curl up for the winter. They sleep under leaves, in rock cracks or in hollow tree trunks. The snoozing bugs may not stir until spring.

Z Z Z Z Z Z

Spring

HOME SWEET HOME

Some moths set up home in a sluggish three-toed sloth's shaggy coat, where it's warm and dry.

Once a week, the sloth climbs down from its tree to go to the toilet. The female moths lay their eggs in the sloth's droppings.

In time, the eggs hatch into larvae which grow into young moths. They fly off to find a sloth to call home.

IDEAL HOME

Great place! I'll move in today.

That's weird

A termite mound has its own air-conditioning system. Chimneys and tunnels run through the mound, drawing in fresh air to help keep the underground nest cool and moist.

Cool man! That's a blast!

▲ This monster-sized mound of mud is built by teeny-weeny termites. Millions of these insects may live in a nest underneath the mound.

That's teamwork

Insects that live in big groups, such as ants and bees, believe in sharing the workload — there are always plenty of jobs to do.

Believe it or not

When a weaver ant finds a new source of food, it leaves a scent trail for its buddies to follow.

I still think cross-stitch looks better.

▲ Weaver ants build their nests with leaves. Some ants hold the edges of a leaf together while others sew it up with a sticky silk made by a young ant. Then the ants attach this leaf to other leaves.

Getting to the bottom of it

Let's dance! When a honeybee finds a supply of its food, called nectar, it flies back to its hive and does a dance with its bottom. The angle of its bottom points in the direction of the food and the type of dance tells the bees how far away it is. A waggly figure-of-eight dance means the nectar is far away.

This way gang!

It's a tough life

A worker bee only lives for about six weeks, but in that time it's all work. Even in the first days of life, the bee has to help around the house.

Day 2

A worker bee's first job is to keep the hive clean.

Day 4

After a few days, it must watch over the newborn bees.

Whaaa!

Day 10

The bee's next job is to make and repair the wax cells that hold food or eggs.

Day 26

After nearly four weeks, the bee is allowed to visit flowers to collect pollen and nectar.

Day 20

Then the bee is put on guard duty to keep a lookout for enemies.

13

A male butterfly is attracted to a female by the patterns and colours of her wings. Some female butterflies also release an irresistible perfume to seduce a partner.

You're my lovebug

Insects woo and court each other in all kinds of romantic ways. They may sing their hearts out, glow beautifully in the dark, or even bring gifts to tempt their loved ones.

That's weird

When male stalk-eyed flies fight over a female, they do it with their eyes! These flies have eyes on long stalks. The male with the longest eyestalks usually wins.

Silken gifts

A male balloon fly spins a huge silk balloon as a present for a female. He flies out with his buddies, each one carrying a balloon, to try to win a fabulous female.

Love is in the air! A male firefly roams the night sky, flashing out a message of love with flickering lights made in its body. A female who likes what she sees flashes back.

Knock! Knock! Who's there?

Finding a partner is head-banging work for deathwatch beetles. When a male wants to meet a mate, he knocks his head against the wooden walls of his home. If a female hears the knocking, she bangs back. It's a date!

I like the sound of him!

A male cricket serenades a mate by rubbing its front wings together to produce loud chirps. The female listens to her many singing suitors before mating with the one whose song she likes best.

Grow up!

Insects start life as eggs, then many go through a series of amazing changes, called metamorphosis. These insects change in appearance completely. Others just grow bigger, shed their skins and eventually sprout wings.

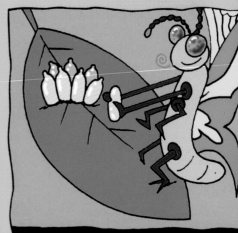

A mother butterfly lays a cluster of tiny eggs and sticks them carefully onto a leaf. Then she flutters off.

Eggs-plosion

A female bomber fly has a sure-fire way of looking after her babies. First she flies in search of her target — a bees' nest on the ground. Then she hovers by the entrance, aims, and fires down her eggs. When the baby flies hatch, they gobble up the unsuspecting baby bees!

Strange but true

Damselflies spend their young lives underwater. They take to the air only when they become adults.

squishy larva, called a ...terpillar, hatches from each egg. ...he caterpillar feasts on yummy ...aves until it grows big and fat.

BURP! Pardon me.

When the caterpillar is full, it finds a comfy spot and makes itself a silky covering. The silk soon hardens into a shell, called a pupa.

My, it's cosy in here!

Yippee! Now I can spread my wings.

Inside the pupa, huge changes take shape. Finally, the pupa splits open as a fully grown butterfly pushes its way out.

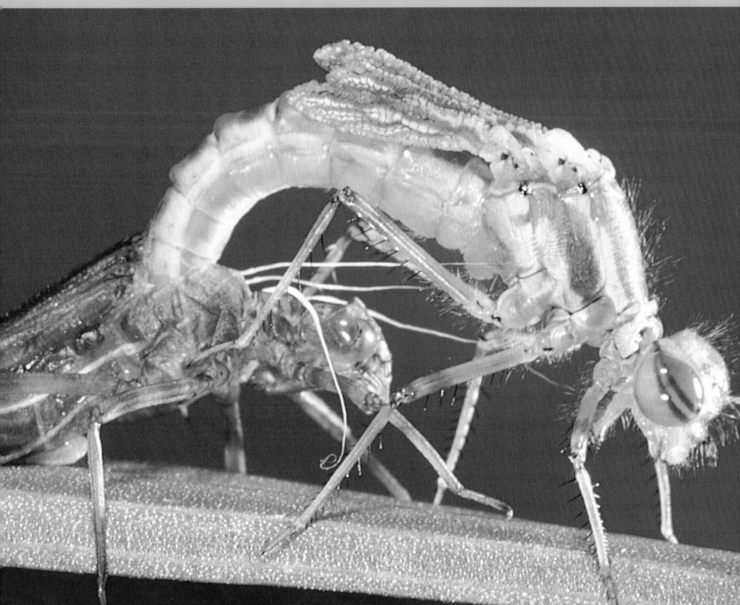

This large red damselfly has grown too big for its skin, so it crawls out of its old skin to reveal a brand new one underneath. The damselfly changes its skin several times as it grows up.

17

What's on the menu?

Watch out for wasps and flies — they like to share your dinner! But many insects munch on juicy leaves or suck sweet nectar juice from flowers. A few bugs prefer totally weird snacks, such as animal droppings.

Dining on droppings

Dung beetles like nothing better than biting into the droppings of elephants or buffalo! First, the beetles shape pieces of dung into balls. Then they roll these stinky balls away. Later, the baby beetles eat the dung for dinner. Yuck!

Spit, suck and slurp

Don't invite a fly to dinner — it has terrible manners. This messy creature spits on its food to turn it into a mushy mess, then slurps up the slop through a pad at the end of its mouth

I just love mashed banana.

▲ Wasps enjoy many of the same foods we do. They happily nibble on meat or fish, and they love to eat sweets and cakes, too.

Hold the knives!

Many insects have special body parts that act as built-in cutlery. A grasshopper's knife-like jaws easily slice up plants, and a butterfly sips flower juices through a long tube, like a straw.

Phew! Nearly there.

A bee doesn't need a shopping trolley to carry food back to its hive. It collects a yummy powder, called pollen, from flowers, and puts it in special baskets on its back legs. At home, the bee feeds the pollen to the young bees.

Heave-ho!

Desert ants use muscle power to lug food home. Just one ant can lift a dead animal up to 50 times its weight. So, if a rat keels over in the scorching desert heat, a hungry ant gang can heave the delicious meal home.

Deadly predators

A few insects are especially fearsome. They use all sorts of dastardly methods to trap their victims, who include fellow creepy-crawlies and even slithery snakes.

DARK DEEDS

What's in a name?

The Malaysian vampire moth feasts on blood, just like Count Dracula. Under cover of night, the moth swoops onto a victim, such as a buffalo, and pierces its skin. Then the bloodsucking bug drinks its fill.

Taking a dive

Creatures that live in water aren't safe from the clever diving beetle. This deadly diver traps a large air bubble beneath its wing cases so that it can breathe underwater, like a scuba diver. Then it hunts for a victim and slices it in half with just one bite.

Uh-oh!

CLOAK AND DAGGER BUG

Eeek!

A Costa Rican assassin bug is a cunning hunter. First the bug finds a lonely, stray termite and stabs it with its dagger-like mouth, sucking the termite dry.

Hungry for more food, the devious assassin bug carries the dried-up termite's body on its back until it reaches a termite mound.

Termites scurry out of the mound to collect their dead comrade — and walk straight into the trap. The beastly bug reveals itself and gobbles them up!

20

Deadly swarm

When African driver ants are on the warpath, other animals better watch out! A swarm of up to 20 million vicious ants marches through the forest. They devour creatures much bigger than themselves, including mice and snakes.

Strange but true

A female praying mantis is deadly — even in love! She's so greedy that she will try to feast on her mate!

A bee is no match for a ferocious praying mantis. This expert killer lies in wait for the passing bee, then pounces, seizing the startled insect in its spiny front legs.

HA HA! Which insect has the smallest appetite? A moth—it just eats holes!

Stand back...

I'm armed and dangerous

Insects have many enemies that want to eat them, so the little creatures find cunning ways to protect themselves. Stingers, prickles and smells are just some of their sneaky weapons.

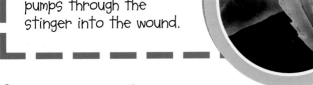

Under the microscope

A bee stinger has sharp barbs that hook into an enemy's skin. Venom pumps through the stinger into the wound.

Chemical warfare

Take cover! A bombardier beetle is like a cannon. It swivels its bottom towards an attacker, then aims and fires with a noisy bang. But, instead of shooting cannonballs, it blasts its attacker with a burning jet of hot chemicals.

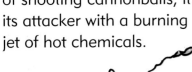

Smelly warnings

Stinkbugs, also called shieldbugs, give off a dreadful stench when threatened. If an attacker ignores the odour and swallows the bug, it won't enjoy its meal — stinkbugs taste as bad as they smell!

This caterpillar is armed with poisonous spines. Bright colours warn enemies to back off or risk a mouthful of prickles and poison.

Tell me how

A CATERPILLAR GLUES ENEMIES TO THE SPOT

A pine sawfly caterpillar seems harmless as it chews pine-tree needles. To a hungry ant, the caterpillar looks like a tasty meal. But the caterpillar has a plan...

...The crafty creature turns the pine-needles into a sticky gum which it spits out. The gum glues the amazed ant to the spot and the caterpillar strolls away to safety.

Fantastic fraudsters

Many insects survive thanks to trickery and cunning. Camouflage is a favourite method of cleverly outwitting dangerous opponents.

▲ At first sight, this looks like a leaf. But look closely and you can see that it's not a leaf at all — it's a deviously disguised leaf insect. Some leaf insects even look like crumpled, rotting leaves!

Getting an eyeful

Moths have markings on their wings that look like giant, scary eyes. These are normally hidden when the insect is resting. But, when a moth senses danger, it flashes its false eyes, scaring the startled predator. This gives the moth enough time to escape from its enemy.

Aaaaagh!

Believe it or not

Insects disguise themselves in all kinds of ways including as twigs, thorns and stones.

That's weird

A harmless wasp beetle puts off predators by looking like a stinging wasp. This master mimic darts across leaves and even flies in the same frantic way as a wasp. What an exhausting act!

I draw the line at buzzing.

No food around here!

Fancy dress

A caddis fly larva has fabulous dress sense. This underwater insect wears pebbles, twigs, weeds and shells — but not for fashion. The larva's many disguises help to keep it safely hidden from hungry fish.

Pesky pests

A handful of insects give other bugs a bad name. They make a real nuisance of themselves by destroying entire fields of crops or munching their way through homes. A few pests even set up house in human hair!

Timber!

Home wreckers

Wood-loving termites eat people out of house and home. They chew away at the inside parts of the timber that holds up a house until only the outer shell of the building is left.

Aargh! What's going on?

Invasion of the crop chompers

Locusts have a huge appetite for crops — one large swarm can strip a farmer's field bare in minutes. A swarm may contain millions of locusts and be so thick that it completely blocks out the sun.

POTATO THIEVES

Mmmm. My favourite — fresh buffalo burweed.

Once upon a time, Colorado beetles were quite content to munch away harmlessly on the delicious leaves of the buffalo burweed.

In the 1800s, the beady-eyed beetles spotted a plant, called the potato, which people had started to grow in nearby fields. Soon this was the beetles' favourite food.

The beetles chomped through the leaves of the potato plants, destroying whole fields of crops. They became major farming pests in the United States, and still are today.

This creature is a head louse. It hooks its claws around human hair so that it can suck the blood from a person's scalp. But don't worry — in real life, this bug is only the size of a pinhead.

27

Little helpers

Most insects are harmless and many are extremely useful. Some produce food or make threads for clothing. Others give farmers and doctors a helping hand. The world would be a poorer place without our buggy buddies.

Ladybirds to the rescue

Farmers and ladybirds are the best of friends. Ladybirds eat tiny aphids that destroy the farmers' crops. These bugs can munch up to 40 aphids a day!

Believe it or not

Young flies, called maggots, were used in hospitals in World War I to heal wounds. They ate the dead skin. Amazing!

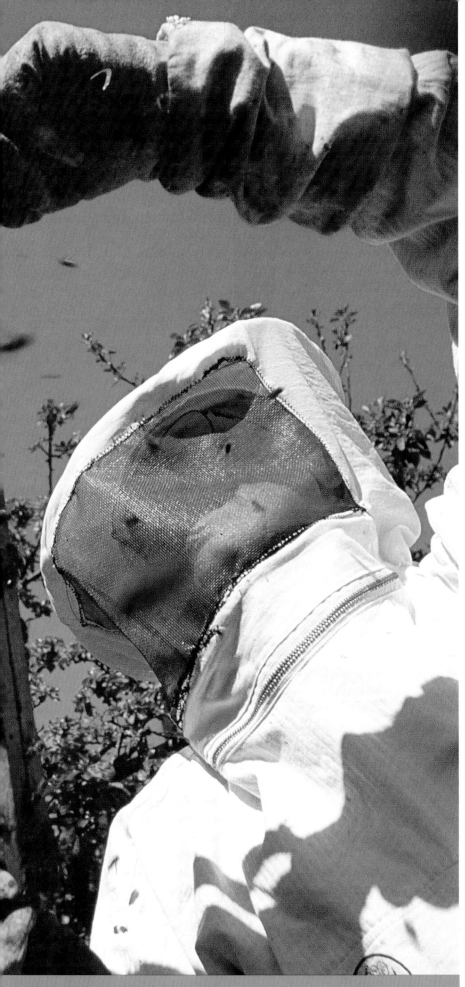

Bees make delicious honey. When beekeepers collect honey from beehives, they wear special suits to guard against bee stings.

Silk makers

Silk clothes are made from thread spun by silkworms. One silkworm can produce an incredibly strong thread almost 600 metres long. Hundreds of these threads are enough to make a super shirt.

Waiter! Waiter! There's a fly in my soup...

Animals aren't the only ones with a taste for insects. You can bite into a mouthwatering mosquito pie in East Africa, devour chocolate-covered ants in North America, and chew on roasted timber beetles in South America — yummy!

Insect superstars

Amazing records abound in the bug world. Look out for the tiniest creatures, the most deafening songsters, and the speediest racers.

Vroooooooom!

...And the dragonfly wins the 90-metre dash, flying in at just over three seconds, easily beating the tropical bee and the hoverfly. The darkling beetle is struggling, crawling in at 90 seconds.

FINISH

Giant jaws

The Australian bulldog ant is one of the fiercest ants in the world. It grabs an insect in its ferociou jaws and delivers a painful sting. Watch out — this ant chases and bites humans, too!

Sticky customer

How's this for size? An African stick insect can grow to 50 centimetres in length — that's over four times the length of a child's hand.

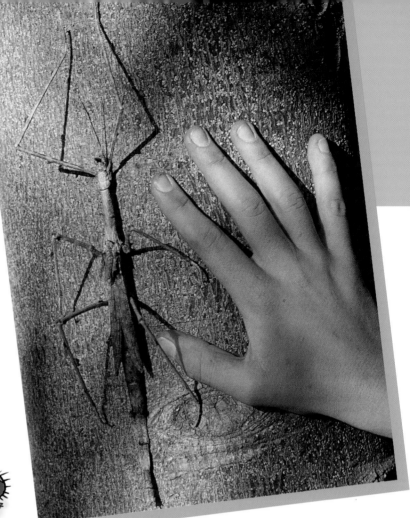

Hearty singers

The prize for noisiness goes to the cicada. The mating song of a male is the world's loudest insect sound. Its buzzing noise can be heard around half a kilometre away.

Can you keep it down?

Teeny-weeny

It's hard to spot a fairy fly — it's one of the smallest insects in the world and is no bigger than the full stop at the end of this sentence.

High jumpers

A flea has a big bounce to its step. It crouches down and springs high into the air. A common cat flea is the champion jumper. It jumps up to 100 times its own height — that would be like you leaping over a 30-storey building.

BOING

WHEEEE

Index

Published by Two-Can Publishing, a division of Zenith Entertainment plc, 43-45 Dorset Street, London W1H 4AB. **www.two-canpublishing.com**

© Two-Can Publishing 2000
For information on Two-Can books and multimedia, call (0)20 7224 2440, fax (0)20 7224 7005, or visit our website at http://www.two-canpublishing.com

Created by act-two, 346 Old Street, London EC1V 9RB

Author: Iqbal Hussain
Illustrations: Gary Boller
Consultant: Jonathan Elphick
Photographs: Front Cover: Still Pictures/Georges Lopez; p1: Oxford Scientific Films; p3: Tony Stone Images; p4: Science Photo Library; pp4-5: Science Photo Library; pp6-7: Fogden Natural History Photographs; p7: Oxford Scientific Films; p8: Planet Earth Pictures; p9: Science Photo Library; p11: Planet Earth Pictures; p12: BBC Natural History Unit; p14: Planet Earth Pictures; pp16-17: Bruce Coleman Ltd; p18: BBC Natural History Unit; pp18-19: Science Photo Library; p21: Oxford Scientific Films; p22: Science Photo Library; pp22-23: Planet Earth Pictures; pp24-25: Oxford Scientific Films; p27: Science Photo Library; p28: Science Photo Library; pp28-29: The Image Bank; p30: Planet Earth Pictures; p31: FLPA.

'Two-Can' is a trademark of Two-Can Publishing.
Two-Can Publishing is a division of Zenith Entertainment plc, 43-45 Dorset Street, London W1H 4AB

ISBN: 1-85434-805-1

10 9 8 7 6 5 4 3 2

Dewey Decimal Classification 595.7

A catalogue record for this book is available from the British Library.

Printed in Hong Kong by Wing King Tong